Table of contents:

Page	Chapter
2.	Introduction and History of the Winchester model 1897
3.	More information from other sources
5.	What to look for when buying a Winchester model 1897
10.	What is my Winchester worth?
12.	Basic disassembly
18.	Winchester exploded view and serial number manufacture dates.
21.	Most common problems of the Winchester model 1897
27.	Extractor angle guide
30.	War Department Technical Manual.

This book was written, and compiled by
William A. Longiotti
(Just Bill)

THE WINCHESTER MODEL 1897 PUMP SHOTGUN

With the popularity of the Winchester '97 shotgun being so heavily used in Cowboy Action Shooting, it has caused the price and demand for this shotgun to increase dramatically. For this reason many people purchase shotguns that should not be fired until repaired. The following information is to help those people and give them a guide on….

"History of the Winchester 1897 Pump Shotgun"
"What to look for when buying a 97 shotgun."
"How to disassemble, clean and reassemble a 97 shotgun."
"Exploded view and manufacture dates"

HISTORY;
The Winchester Pump Shotgun was designed by John Browning. It was first designated as the Model 1893 Slide-Action. In 1890 Winchester bought the Browning design, hoping to capture the market that the Spencer and Burgess Shotgun companies had already introduced. John Browning had designed an outside-hammer gun with ejection to the side. I will not cover anymore information on the 1893 shotgun, due to the fact this shotgun was design only for black powder and with the introduction of smokeless powder, improvements had to be made to the existing shotgun. The Model 1897 was first listed for sale in the November 1897 Winchester catalog as a 12 gauge solid frame. However, the 12 gauge takedown was added in October 1898, and the 16 gauge takedown in February 1900. The Model 1897 Shotgun became an instant hit. The 1897 became the best-known and widely used exposed hammer, side-action gun in history. This gun was offered in numerous barrel lengths and grades, chambered in 12 and 16 gauges, and as a solid frame or takedown. The 16-gauge guns had a standard barrel length of 28 inches, while 12-gauge guns were furnished with 30-inch length barrels. Most if not all 30 inch barrels and longer were made with a full choke. If you see a shorter barrel with a full choke imprint most likely it has been cut. Special length barrels could be ordered in lengths as short as 20 inches, and as long as 36 inches. The model 1897 trigger sear has no disconnector. This allows the shotgun to be fired rapidly; by holding the trigger back and operating the slide as quickly as the shooter can. (This is sometimes referred to as "slam firing"). This ability and its six-shot capacity made it extremely effective for close combat, with devastating results.

Since the time the Model 1897 was first manufactured it has been used by American soldiers, police departments, hunters and now Cowboy Action shooters. The Model 1897 was discontinued in 1957. It was produced for an amazing 60 years.

The Chinese company Norinco has made an effort to reproduce this firearm. It has also been produced under other company names. The imported Chinese 97 is an almost exact copy of the solid frame Winchester 1897, produced mostly for the cowboy action shooters. When first introduced, many thought it would be a better shotgun than the original. With new metallurgy, better milling equipment (CNC equipment) to cut and fit parts and joints together, most people felt this new 1897 shotgun would exceed the quality and durability of the original Winchester model 1897.

As the years have past we find this just isn't true. The imported 97 lacks in the fit, finish, and the durability (over 120 years of use) of the originals. I am seeing the imported shotguns with rough milling, burrs in the bearing surfaces and sloppy fit where a tight fit is required.

More information obtained from other sources.

The Winchester 1897 shotgun is an exposed hammer, pump operated shotgun. The forearm was made originally with circular grooves around it. Later models change the forearm configuration. One nickname for this gun was the "cornshucker"

The model 1893 was the predecessor to the 1897, with about 33,000 being made. It originally used 2 1/2" ammo. It was also only made in the solid frame. (no take down). It can be readily identified by the unusual opening on the top of the receiver.

A & B Series:

In June 1897, the model 1897 was born & the following changes were made to the 1893. Then the gun was called the Model 1897, with the serial numbers of the guns continuing from the 1893. Apparently the series A & B relate to the 1893. Not sure if all "B" guns had rounded end magazine plugs.

(1) New firing pin lock put in breech block.
(2) Screw put in receiver to hold magazine from turning.
(3) Release pin and plunger (for action slide lock)
(4) Top of cartridge ejecting opening in frame made straight.
(5) Spring placed on inside of action handle encircling magazine.
(6) Collar put inside of magazine to keep spring and follower from coming out.
(7) Top of breech block made straight.
(8) Receiver holding bolt made shorter.
(9) Butt stock made longer, drop changed, and outside shape changed slightly.
(10) Friction spring put in under cartridge guide.

C Series:

In February 1898, after about 47,000 shotguns had been made, more changes were made in the Model 1897. After that date the gun was marked with the letter "C" over the serial number.

(1) A small wire was put into the receiver and connected to the action slide lock release pin, to hold it from coming out when the gun was taken apart.
(2) Receiver made 1 1/2 (one and one half) hundredths??? Thicker on each side. This was thought best on account of the increased cuts on the inside.
(3) Action slide lock spring was changed.
(4) The first Model 1897's had no ejector spring. (The ejector was a little block pinned to the LH receiver wall.) This spring is a small thin "L" shaped spring with a screw hole that is attached from the outside LH side of the receiver immediately in front of the "ejector".

D Series:

The end of the magazine plug was flat on "D" guns.

E Series:

In April 1898, after about 50,000 shotguns had been made (Model 1893 & 1897) some more changes were made, and the model 1897 detachable barrel and magazine put on the market. These were known as the "E" series guns.

"E" guns had slightly deeper 5/16 wide grooves on the receiver ring.

Prior to "E" guns, cartridge stops were fastened with screws through the receiver sides and shells were difficult to release from the magazine. For unloading, most shooters worked them through the action. On E models, the cartridge stops fastened through the bottom of the action and providing buttons which could be pushed to retract the cartridge stops.

These are not all the changes. Madis stated that 37 major and 52 minor changes were made in the first 12 years of production of the Model 1897.

Other items that may be of some interest:

1. Standard shotgun stock was 13 3/4 inches.
2. Frame altered on 1897 to use 2 3/4" ammo.
3. Brush gun was made available November 1897 to 1931. It had shorter stock with more drop and 26 inch barrel.
4. Standard gun was made with rolled steel barrels, full choke standard. Cylinder or modified choke on special order.
5. Standard barrel length 30 or 32 inch. 30 inch shipped if not specified.
6. Trap Gun 12 and 16 gauge (1897 to 1931). The gun had 30 inch rolled steel barrel, select fancy walnut handmade stock. Straight checked grip with oil finish and black diamonds in the grip, and checked rubber butt plate. It was first listed at $47.
7. Trap Gun was engraved on the breech block and could be had with matted barrel.
8. Within certain limits, purchasers could specify stock dimensions.
9. Solid frame and takedown trap guns were made. After 1926 Trap Gun was not always engraved on the breech block.
10. Receivers on Trap, Tournament, Pigeon, Standard Trap, and Special Trap guns had matted groove.

What to look for when buying a Winchester 1897

The first thing to do is make sure the gun is unloaded.
Then give attention to the general overall condition.
Is all the bluing gone? Are there any dents in the barrel? Is the magazine tube dent free.
Has somebody damaged the barrel with a pipe wrench, or by hammering on the receiver?
Now let's check the details….
Check the magazine to see if the slide stop is on top.

If not, someone assembled it incorrectly. This will cause a poor fit and it will be difficult to assemble and disassemble.

Next open the action. Check to see if the left hand extractor is broken.

The extractor spring leg should be visible. Check that the firing pin lock screw is tight, and look at the condition of the ejector spring.

While the action is still open, check the carrier.

Check the action slide groove. Is it worn? Check the Action slide lock, (that little thin metal piece). Is it rounded too much? Is it bent? Make sure it can be pushed in and springs out.

Now turn the action around. Look inside to see the ejector spring leg.

The ejector spring leg should be visible and the hole should not be clogged with any foreign matter. The left hand extractor should also be visible.

Now close the action and look at the back of the carrier (below the hammer)

Check the carrier stop screw. Is it broken, stripped?
Is the slot stripped? If this is the case, you will have problems disassembling the shotgun, and it will cost money to have it removed professionally.

While you are back there check the bolt slide tracks on the receiver.
This one has the bluing worn off but the tracks are clean and in good shape

Sometimes people have pounded on them trying to make the bolt stay down to cock the hammer. This is not good.

Determine if the receiver is an early, or a late model?

The top receiver is a newer model. It has buttons that can be pushed from the **<u>outside</u>** to release the cartridges in the magazine.

The lower receiver is the older one. It utilizes a cartridge release that requires it to be pushed **<u>inside</u>** of the receiver to release the cartridges without running them through the chamber. This really doesn't affect the firearm one way or the other, but is something to be aware of. Unloading a full magazine is a little more difficult.

Check the choke on the gun.

The main purpose of this is simple. A full choke gun was manufactured with a long barrel. If the gun says "Full" and it has a short barrel less than 26 inches, you can bet it was cut. If it says "Mod" it will be most of the time, a 26 or 24 inch barrel.
If it says "Cyl" It was manufactured with a short barrel.
I give you this information to help you determine if the barrel has been cut or not.
If you are buying it because you want a short barrel gun, then it may not matter.
However it is always good to assess what work has been done to modify a firearm.
Now is a good time to grab the barrel with one hand and the stock with the other and wiggle it. Does the barrel feel loose? If so the bushing may need adjusting or replacing.

Open the action slowly and then close the action slowly. Make sure the hammer stays in the cocked position. If the hammer follows the bolt down, then something needs repaired. It could be something simple, or very costly. Beware.

Now check the condition of the wood.

Check the wood on the action slide. Is it broken, cracked or some pieces missing?
This could cost you at least $50.00 to replace.
How is the wood butt stock? Is it cracked? Can it be repaired? Does it have a rubber butt pad? If so, it has been added. Has the butt stock been shortened?
This could be a problem if you have long arms.
If you have to replace the butt stock it can cost as much as $75.00. Take all of this into consideration.

Many times I have been asked **"What is my Winchester model 97 worth?"**
Or
"How much should I pay for a Winchester model 97?"

Many years ago I remember an elderly gentleman gave me an answer to a similar question.
He said let me answer this with a question.
"How long is a rope?"
With that I asked **"WHAT?"**
He started out telling me there are too many variables. Then he started listing them:
Here is my rendition of his answer relating it to a firearm.

1. What kind of condition is it in?

A. Is it new in the original box?
B. Is it only slightly worn?
C. Has it been used as a hammer (is it beaten up)?
D. Does it have only honest wear?
E. Has it been restored?
F.

2. What do you want to do with it?

A. Do you going to keep it and never shoot it?
B. Maybe you want to only shoot it once a year.
C. Do you want to duck hunt with it?
D. Do you want it for a truck gun (leave it in the truck)?
E. Are you looking to used it as a cowboy Action Shooting firearm?

3. Where are you located?

A. Some location the Winchester model 97 is in demand
B. Some locations there are an abundance of them with very little demand.

4. Do you want this gun and can you afford it?

A. I have always stated "With any firearm, if you want the gun and you are going to enjoy it, shoot it, have fun with it, and you have the finances to purchase it,
THEN BY ALL MEANS GET THE GUN.
B. This doesn't mean you pay two or 3 times the value, No, it just means buy the gun shoot it, have fun with it, and cherish it.
REMEMBER COST IS ONLY RELATIVE TO EVERY THING ELSE.

Note: This next information is only here to help you evaluate the shotgun.
It still won't tell you if the shotgun will fire safely, if the chamber needs lengthening, or if any other internal parts need replacing.
The 1897 shotgun has more parts than any other shotgun.
Remember it should always be checked out by a competent gunsmith.

PLEASE READ THIS BEFORE ATEMPTING TO WORK ON ANY FIREARM.

This booklet is to be used only as a **reference**. Not every problem or cure will be in this reference. There could be other factors at issue. If you are not sure how to unload and check the action of a Winchester model 97, or are unsure how it functions, please do not attempt any repairs.

A qualified gunsmith can assist you, and can do all the repairs you need. You must always be safe when handling and working on any firearm. Check to see if the firearm is empty and the action is open. Then check the firearm again. Once a firearm has had an accidental discharge, there is nothing you can do to bring back that bullet or shot back. **It will be too late.**

Never have live ammo around you when working on a firearm. Use only empty or dummy rounds. I will repeat this statement….. **Never have live ammo around you when working on a firearm. Use only empty or dummy rounds.**

If you do decide to work on your own firearm, it recommended to have a qualified gunsmith check out the firearm, to be sure your work was done correctly.

Basic disassembly
Let's start out with the solid frame disassembly.

Remove the screw holding the magazine tube,

After the screw is removed, slide the magazine band off the barrel.

Remove the screw on the receiver.

Turn the magazine counter clockwise to unscrew the magazine tube

From here on, the disassembly is the same as the takedown model.

For the takedown 97 model push the pin located at the end of the magazine tube

**Rotate the pin and magazine counter clockwise ¼ turn.
Grab the slide and push up towards the end of the magazine tube. This will expose the threads of the magazine. And release the action slide.**

Twist the barrel and magazine tube assembly approximately ¼ turn or slightly more. Counter clockwise

This will allow the barrel to be pulled out of the receiver.

From here on disassemble is the same for the solid and takedown frame. Remove carrier stop screw

Take care in removing screw. If you strip it, only a gunsmith can remove it without damage.

Push out the carrier pin

It will not need to be driven out. Just push it with a small screwdriver

Remove cartridge guide stop screw

Note the screw has a small unthreaded end on it.

With the hammer in the down position push the carrier down through the bottom of the action.

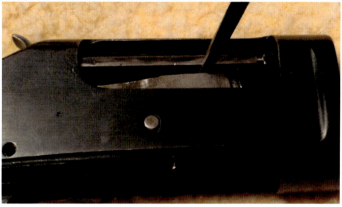

**As you pull down on the carrier, pull the hammer back to full cock.
The carrier should pull out with no difficult.**

Remove action slide hook screw

**Do not ever remove the small screw to the right.
There is another screw just like it on the other side.
They hold the barrel chamber ring. If it is removed,
the chamber must be realigned. This is not an easy job.**

Turn the shotgun horizontal shake out the action slide hook

Pull the bolt out the back of the receiver.

At this point the shotgun is torn down sufficient for cleaning. Do not dissemble any farther. The parts can be cleaned and oiled. To reassemble just reverse the procedure. Specialize tools are required to strip the bolt and carrier further.

You should have the following parts;
1. One stripped receiver.
2. One complete breach bolt.
3. One complete carrier.
4. One action slide hook screw.
5. One carrier pin.
6. One carrier pin stop screw.
7. One carrier guide stop screw.
8. One action hook.

The following pages have the 1897 Winchester disassembled parts and their names. Included also are the serial numbers assigned at the end of each calendar year the shotgun was manufactured.

Thanks to Thomas Wessel for the detail drawing of the Model 1897 Slide Action Shotgun.

Mr. Pat Redmond also researched and compiled the information on the Trench gun and their serial numbers.

The author with his favorite Winchester model 1897

Model 1897 Slide-Action Shotgun

Courtesy of Thomas E. Wessel

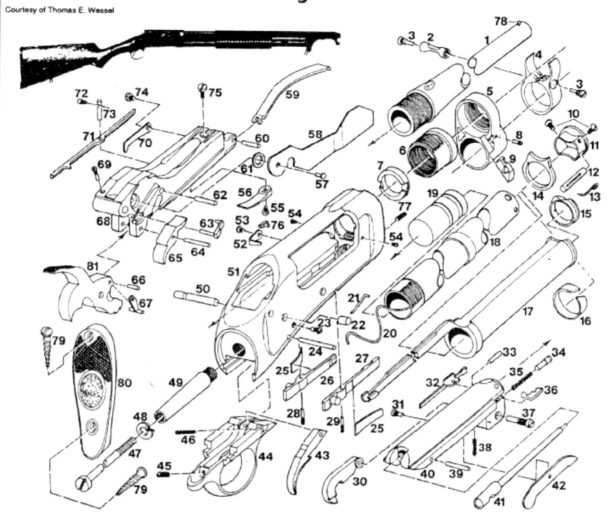

KEY

1. Barrel
2. Magazine Band Bushing
3. Magazine Band Bushing Screws
4. Magazine Band
5. Barrel Extension
6. Adjusting Sleeve
7. Barrel Chamber Ring
8. Adjusting Sleeve Lock Screw
9. Adjusting Sleeve Lock
10. Magazine Plug Screws
11. Magazine End Cap
12. Magazine Locking Pin
13. Magazine Locking Pin Spring
14. Magazine End Cap Stop
15. Action Slide Sleeve Screw Cap
16. Action Slide Spring
17. Action Slide
18. Magazine Tube
19. Magazine Follower
20. Magazine Spring
21. Action Slide Lock Release Plunger Pin Spring
22. Action Slide Lock Release Plunger Pin
23. Cartridge Guide Stop Screw
24. Trigger Pin
25. Cartridge Stop Springs
26. Cartridge Stop, Left
27. Cartridge Stop, Right
28. Cartridge Stop Screw, Left
29. Cartridge Stop Screw, Right
30. Action Slide Hook
31. Firing Pin Lock Screw
32. Extractor, Left
33. Extractor Pin, Left
34. Extractor Plunger, Right
35. Extractor Plunger Spring, Right
36. Extractor, Right
37. Action Slide Hook Screw
38. Firing Pin Lock Spring
39. Firing Pin Stop Pin
40. Breechbolt
41. Firing Pin
42. Firing Pin Lock
43. Trigger
44. Guard Bow
45. Trigger Stop Screw
46. Trigger Spring
47. Buttstock Bolt
48. Buttstock Bolt Washer
49. Receiver Shank
50. Carrier Pin
51. Receiver
52. Ejector Spring
53. Ejector Spring Screw
54. Barrel Chamber Ring Retaining Screws
55. Sear Spring Screw
56. Sear Spring
57. Cartridge Guide Rivet
58. Cartridge Guide
59. Mainspring
60. Mainspring Pin
61. Cartridge Guide Friction Spring
62. Hammer Pin
63. Action Slide Lock Release Plunger
64. Sear Pin
65. Sear
66. Hammer Stirrup Pin
67. Hammer Stirrup
68. Carrier
69. Carrier Pin Stop Screw
70. Action Slide Lock Spring
71. Action Slide Lock
72. Action Slide Lock Joint Pin Stop Screw
73. Action Slide Lock Joint Pin
74. Action Slide Lock Spring Screw
75. Mainspring Strain Screw
76. Ejector Pin
77. Extension Stop Screw
78. Front Sight
79. Buttplate Screws
80. Buttplate
81. Hammer

Parts Not Shown
Action Slide Handle
Buttstock

RECORDS AT THE FACTORY INDICATE THE FOLLOWING SERIAL NUMBERS WERE ASSIGNED TO GUNS AT THE END OF THE CALENDAR YEAR.

MODEL 1897

Year	Serial No.	Year	Serial No.
1897 -	1 TO 32335	1928 -	796806
98 -	64668	29 -	807321
99 -	96999	30 -	812729
1900 -	129332	31 -	830721
01 -	161665	32 -	833926
02 -	193998	33 -	835637
03 -	226331	34 -	837364
04 -	258664	35 -	839728
05 -	296037	36 -	848684
06 -	334059	37 -	856729
07 -	377999	38 -	860725
08 -	413618	39 -	866938
09 -	446888	40 -	875945
10 -	481062	41 -	891190
11 -	512632	42 -	910072
12 -	544313	43 -	912265
13 -	575213	44 -	912327
14 -	592732	45 -	916472
15 -	607673	46 -	926409
16 -	624537	47 -	936682
17 -	646124	48 -	944085
18 -	668383	49 -	953042
19 -	691943	50 -	961999
20 -	696183	51 -	970956
21 -	700428	52 -	979913
22 -	715902	53 -	988860
23 -	732060	54 -	997827
24 -	744942	55 -	1006784
25 -	757629	56 -	1015741
26 -	770527	57 -	1024700
27 -	783574		

RECORDS ON THIS MODEL ARE INCOMPLETE. THE ABOVE SERIAL NUMBERS ARE ESTIMATED FROM 1897 THRU 1903 AND AGAIN FROM 1949 THRU 1957. THE ACTUAL RECORDS ARE IN EXISTANCE FROM 1904 THROUGH 1949.

MODEL 1897 TRENCH/RIOT SHOTGUN

This information is provided by Mr. Pat Redmond. After many years of research and collecting. Reference a Winchester Repeating Arms Co. Memorandum dated September 1945. Trench, Riot, and Long Barrel Contract Dates 1/31/42 - 3/23/43, Contract Shipments 24829 shotguns.

Year	Ser. Nos.	Type Configuration
1937	902117-903762	Mil. Long Barrel
1939	911788-911813	Mil. Trench Gun
1940	914087	Com. Trench Gun
1940	924312	Com. Trench Gun
1941	920235-956126	Mil. Trench Gun
1942	930537-956216	Mil. Trench Gun
1943	956628	Mil. Trench Gun
1944	965482	Com. Trench Gun
1944	966144	Com. Trench Gun
1944	967371	Com. Riot Gun
1949	993750	Com. Riot Gun

The most common problems of the Winchester model 97 and their repairs. I am going to repeat this paragraph because of its importance.

PLEASE READ THIS BEFORE ATEMPTING TO WORK ON ANY FIREARM.

This booklet is to be used only as a **reference**. Not every possible problem or repair will be covered in this reference. There could be other factors at issue. If you are unsure how to unload and check the action of a Winchester model 97, unsure how it functions, or disassembles, please do not attempt any repairs.
A qualified gunsmith can assist you, and can do all the repairs you need. You must always be safe when handling and working on any firearm. Check to see if the firearm is empty and the action is open. Then check the firearm again. Once a firearm has had an accidental discharge, there is nothing you can do to bring back that bullet. **It will be too late.**
Never have live ammo around you when working on a firearm. Use only empty or dummy rounds. I will repeat this statement..... **Never have live ammo around you when working on a firearm. Use only empty or dummy rounds.**

If you do decide to work on your own firearm, it is recommended to have a qualified gunsmith check out your repairs; to be sure your work was done correctly.

Problem: The cartridge guide, (cartridge flag), doesn't rise when the action is fully open and starts to close.

Cause: The cartridge guide screw is missing or has been replaced with an improper screw.

Repair: Remove the cartridge guide screw.
Look at the screw to see if it is the correct screw.
It should have a stepped down shaft on it.
If not, replace it with the correct screw.

Problem: When the trigger is pulled, the hammer has a small catch as it falls.

Cause: Worn sear, worn trigger.

Repair: Remove rear wood stock. Adjust the trigger stop screw by turning it counterclockwise 1/8th turn.

Test hammer. If it is still catching, turn trigger stop screw counterclockwise another 1/8 turn. **Test again.** <u>*Do not remove or turn trigger stop screw excessively.*</u>

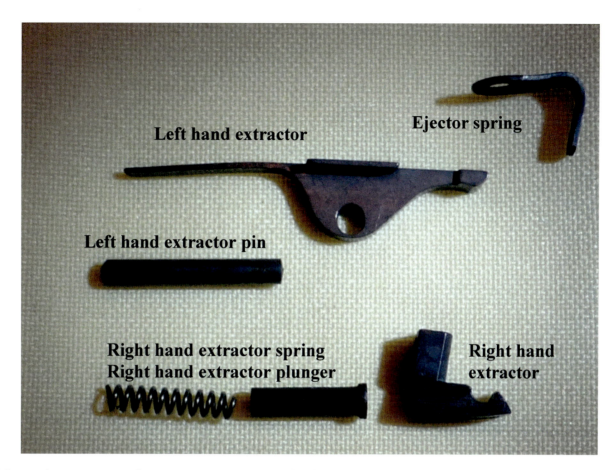

At this point I am going to get more technical, and perhaps a little boring. I am going a different direction then most. I have never seen anyone try to explain the extraction and ejection process of the Winchester model 97 this way before. I may be totally off base, but let's see where this ends up.
You will need a trigger scale and a once fired 12 gauge shot shell. Cut down the shot shell to a total length of 1 1/2 inches.
We will start with the ejector spring. The ejector spring leg must be a few thousands smaller than the hole (remember it must be able to move forward and backwards). If necessary shave the leg narrower. When tightening the screw, make sure the side of the ejector spring is not coming in contact with hole.

Next, look on the inside of the receiver. The leg of the ejector should show clearance all around the hole. See next photo...

In this photo you can see the ejector pin and the leg of the ejector. The ejector is centered with clearance all around the hole. This allows the ejector to move freely back and forward.

Let's move to the next step.

Here you will use the trigger scale. Place the portion that lies on the trigger and put it on the inside of the receiver. Pull on the ejector spring until it moves back, but not touching the ejector pin. Make a note of how many pounds of pull. Remember the left hand extractor must hold the empty shell tight enough to move the ejector spring back. When the left hand extractor releases, the spring will push the empty shot shell out. Note: the tighter the left hand extractor has to hold the empty shell, the harder you must pull back on the action slide to eject the round.

The bolt with the right and left hand extractors is the next thing we work on. The shell should be held in place by the extractors.

Place the empty, once fired, cut down shot shell on the face of the bolt. The cartridge should be held in place on its own...You are using an empty shell; however the bolt should be able to hold the weight of a fully loaded shell.

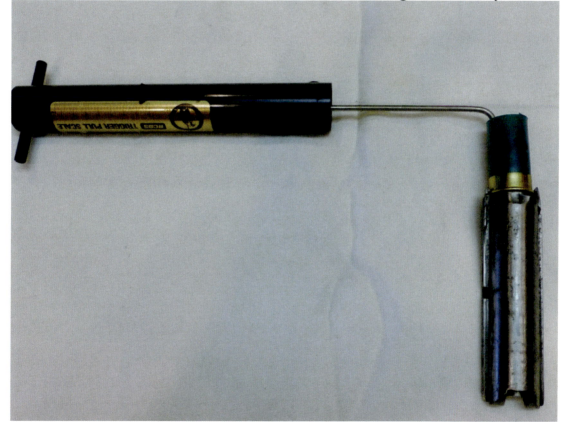

Place the scale's trigger finger into the empty shot shell. With the bolt facing up, pull the scale to the left; testing the right hand extractor. It should not release even up to 12 pounds or more pull. The right hand extractor should have a positive cut to the edge. That means it should not release easily. If it releases easily, reshape the extractor using a file or stone. Be careful not to over cut and ruin the extractor.

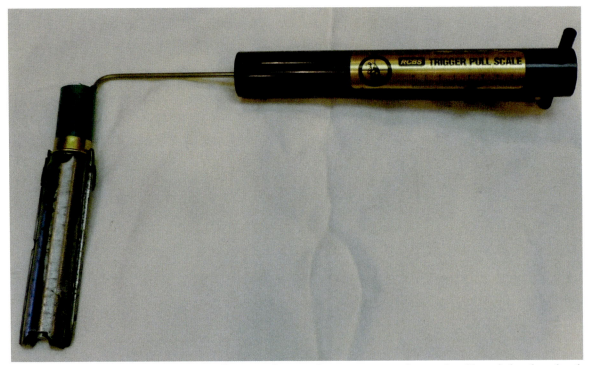

Next, place the scale's trigger finger into the empty shot shell with the bolt facing up.

Pull the scale to the right and make note of how many pounds it takes to release the empty shot shell. Here is where I probably will get into trouble with my theory. OH WELL, HERE IT GOES. Remember when you tested the ejector spring? Let's say it came out at 7 pounds. This means the left hand extractor must hold that empty shot shell to somewhere around 6 to 7 pounds. That allows the shot shell the ability to use all of the built up energy of the ejector spring. If the left hand extractor releases at 3 pounds, you can understand why the shell won't eject well. At that point you are relying on the energy of your arm to pull the action slide back rapidly to eject the shell. The ejector spring is not even being put to use. There is a catch to all of this: The harder the ejector spring is to flex, the harder the left hand extractor has to hold the shell. Be aware, this results in the action slide having to pull harder at the end of the stroke. I feel by making the ejector spring thinner, the left hand extractor can be matched much easier.

The left hand extractor is normally cut to neutral. This may have to be slightly altered to increase the hold of the left hand extractor. See the next page for examples of extractor cuts.

Here again, don't go crazy. Use only one or two sweeps with a fine file.

POSITIVE EXTRACTOR HOOK ANGLE

All right hand extractors will have a positive hook angle.
With the extractor in the "WORKING POSITION" (ie; the extractor is pushing against the case and holding it up against the bolt face).

Line A = a line parallel to the extractor hook angle
Line B = a line parallel to the rim of the cartridge case.

POSITIVE EXTRACTOR HOOK ANGLE
Line A angles away from line B

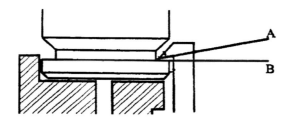

NEUTRAL EXTRACTOR HOOK ANGLE
Line A parallels line B

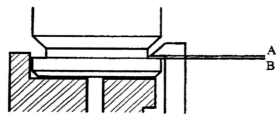

NEGATIVE EXTRACTOR HOOK ANGLE
Line A angles towards and crosses line B

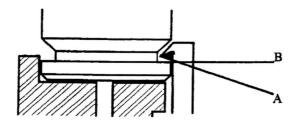

When ever you are removing or reshaping a part, **Always go slowly.** Use a fine file or a stone. Take two or three strokes, then put the part back together and test. It is always easy to remove metal, but putting it back on is tougher. I hope the information I have compiled here will be of help to you. Remember there is always a different way to do things. What worked for me, may not for you. If you bring in two or three gunsmiths and ask them a question you can get three or even four different answers.

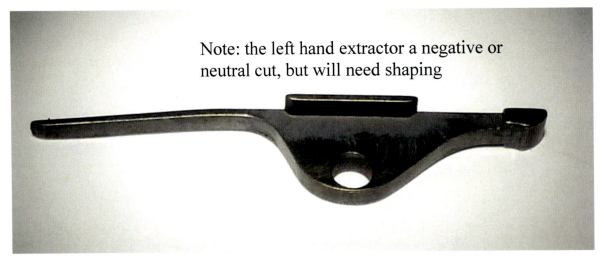

Note: the left hand extractor a negative or neutral cut, but will need shaping

Note: the right hand extractor should have a positive cut

Problem: Barrel on takedown model 97 is loose.

Cause: Worn adjusting sleeve.

Repair: Remove barrel check adjusting sleeve if some adjustment is left loosen adjusting sleeve screw. Slide adjusting slide lock back. Turn adjusting sleeve one notch tighten all the parts, put barrel back on and test for tightness. Note: if barrel can't be adjusted the adjusting sleeve may be too worn. If you can fine new ones it may need to be replaced. Winchester made the adjusting sleeves without numbers and also made adjusting sleeves numbered 1- 5. They used a slightly different pitch to take up the looseness and tighten up the barrel. Some outfits are selling thin brass shims to fill up the space between the barrel and action. This is not the proper way to repair the problem.

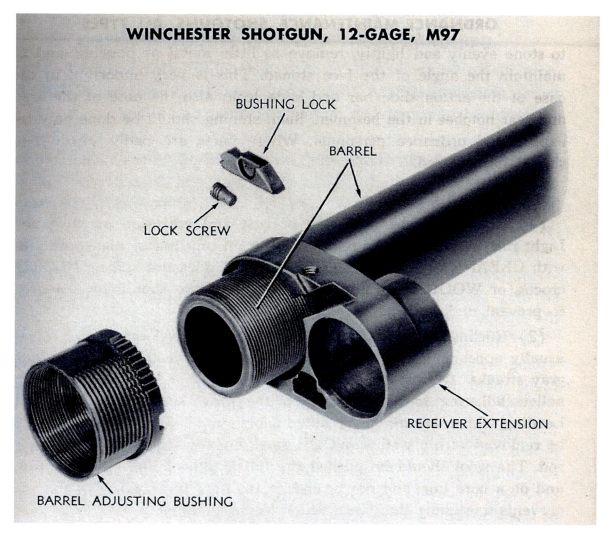

For those that can't get enough information about the Winchester Model 1897

**The following pages have been obtained from;
TM 9-1285
War Department
Technical Manual
Ordnance Maintenance
Shotguns November 25, 1942**

**This book was written in 1942, over 74 years ago, and has not been in production since.
The information found here is interesting and fun to read.**

You may even learn something.

Section II

WINCHESTER SHOTGUN, 12-GAGE, M97

	Paragraph
Description	4
Data	5
Operation	6
Functioning	7
Disassembly and assembly	8
Field inspection	9
Maintenance and repair	10
Cleaning and lubrication	11

4. DESCRIPTION.

a. Identification Marks. Identification marks on this gun are generally to be found as follows:

(1) Name of maker, gage, model and barrel boring are stamped on the top of the barrel near the breech end.

(2) Serial number of the gun is stamped on the lower face of the barrel near the breech end, and on the lower face of the forward end of the receiver.

(3) On solid frame gun, maker's name and model are stamped on the action slide bar, and the serial number of the gun, as in (2) above.

b. This gun (figs. 1 and 2) is a manually operated repeating shotgun of the slide-action, hammer type. All riot guns with bayonets, as well as some other guns of early manufacture are solid frame (fig. 1). Sporting guns of later manufacture are take-down guns (fig. 2). In the solid frame gun the barrel is screwed into the receiver at manufacture and is not intended to be removed except for replacement; the magazine is also screwed into the receiver but can easily be removed by removing a stop screw and by unscrewing the magazine from the receiver. The take-down gun is so constructed that the barrel and magazine, together with the action slide group, can easily be removed as a unit by disengaging interrupted threads on rear end of the magazine and barrel from like interrupted threads in the receiver, by which the barrel and magazine are locked to the receiver. This construction facilitates cleaning and transportation of the gun.

c. Both designs of this gun are furnished in various grades, having barrels of different length and degrees of boring and other modifications of design. Basically, however, the mechanism of the guns is identical except for the differences in design mentioned in **b** above. For convenience, the guns will be classified as three types: riot, skeet, and sporting, although variations of these types may occur.

TM 9-1285

ORDNANCE MAINTENANCE, SHOTGUNS, ALL TYPES

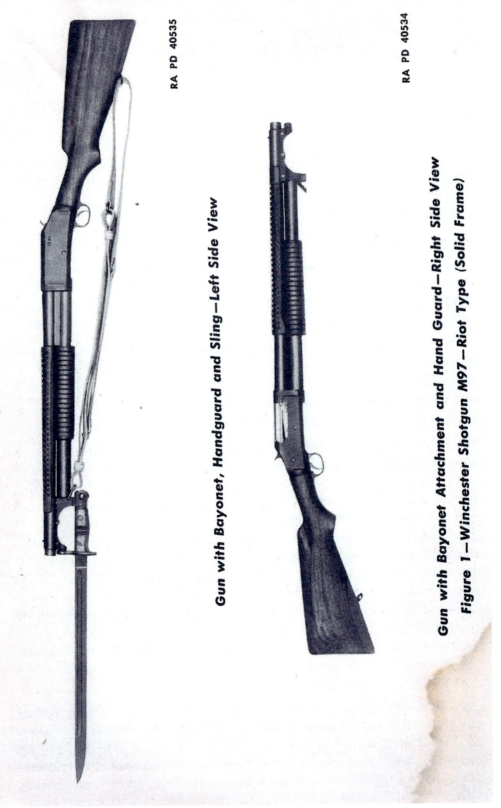

Gun with Bayonet, Handguard and Sling—Left Side View

Gun with Bayonet Attachment and Hand Guard—Right Side View

Figure 1—Winchester Shotgun M97—Riot Type (Solid Frame)

TM 9-1285
4

WINCHESTER SHOTGUN, 12-GAGE, M97

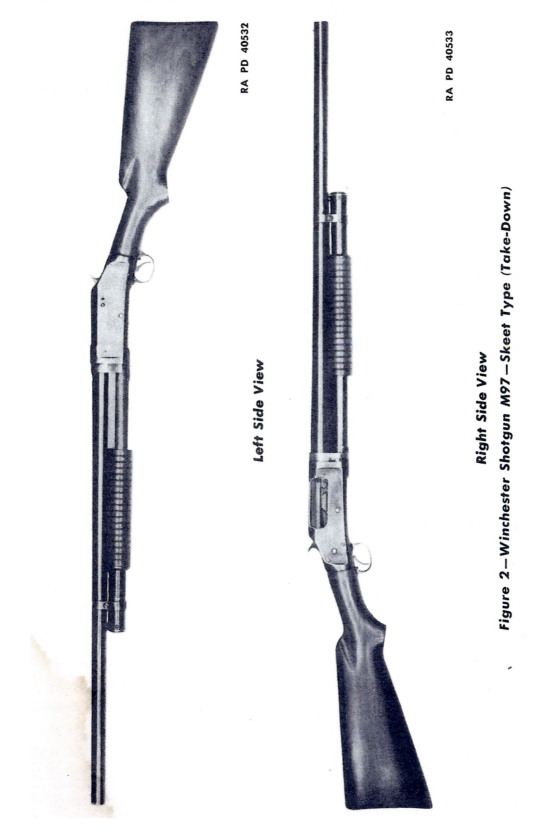

RA PD 40532 — Left Side View
RA PD 40533 — Right Side View

Figure 2 — Winchester Shotgun M97 — Skeet Type (Take-Down)

ORDNANCE MAINTENANCE, SHOTGUNS, ALL TYPES

(1) The riot type gun (fig. 1) may come in either the solid frame or take-down design, with a 20-inch plain barrel, bored (full) cylinder. Some of these guns have a bayonet attachment and hand guard (fig. 4) attached to the muzzle end of the barrel and the magazine, and a leather sling attached to a sling swivel on the bayonet attachment and the stock.

(2) The skeet type gun (fig. 2) usually comes in the take-down design only and is furnished with a 26-inch plain or ribbed barrel, bored improved cylinder, and is without bayonet attachment or sling.

(3) The sporting type gun is similar to the skeet type gun but is furnished with a 30-inch barrel, bored full choke, and is without bayonet attachment or sling.

d. General Description (figs. 5 and 6).

(1) The stock of the gun is bolted to the rear end of the receiver, and the barrel and magazine are fastened to the forward end of the receiver in either of the ways expained in **b** above. The action slide is mounted and operates on the magazine. The rear end of the slide, or bar, passes through the forward end of the receiver and engages with, and cam-operates the carrier pivoted in the receiver, and at the same time reciprocates the breech bolt through the medium of a hook pivoted on the bolt (fig. 3).

(2) The receiver contains the operating mechanism and to its lower rear end is attached the trigger plate in which the trigger is mounted. The receiver is open at the bottom to permit loading, at the rear to permit rearward passage of the breech bolt, and at the right side for ejection of the fired shell cases.

(3) The breech bolt contains the firing pin and lock, and the extractors. The carrier contains the hammer, sear and action slide lock, together with their springs and components. The trigger plate contains the trigger, trigger spring, and stop screw. The ejector is mounted to the left wall of the receiver, and the action slide lock release plunger pin is mounted in the right wall of the receiver.

(4) There is no trigger safety on this gun, this function being performed by setting the hammer at the half cock which prevents retraction of the trigger and release of the action slide.

(5) The magazine, which is of the tubular type, is positioned beneath the barrel and has a capacity of five shells loaded end to end. The shells are pressed together and fed into the receiver by the force of the magazine spring acting upon the follower.

(6) The shell-stops are located in the lower forward inside wall of the receiver and act to hold the shells in the magazine against the pressure of the magazine spring. The stops are operated by the carrier

WINCHESTER SHOTGUN, 12-GAGE, M97

to release and block the shells at the proper time, thus allowing but one shell to enter the receiver at a time.

(7) The action slide lock (fig. 3) is positioned in the left side of the carrier and acts upon the action slide (bar) to block its rearward movement after the breech bolt is locked in position by the carrier, thereby preventing premature unlocking of the bolt. The lock is disengaged either by the descending hammer, pressing on the action slide lock release plunger, when the gun is fired, or by manual pressure on the action slide lock release plunger pin. When the lock is disengaged from the rear end of the action slide bar, the slide may be moved to the rear to cam-down the carrier, unlock the bolt, and function the operating mechanism.

(8) The bayonet attachment and hand guard, common to the riot type gun only, are riveted together and mounted on the muzzle end of the barrel and forward end of the magazine, and are held in place by means of a lug on the magazine plug and screws passing through the attachment and grooves in the barrel. A sling swivel is attached to the attachment and stock, respectively, and supplies the means for fastening the sling to the gun.

(9) The gun sling is leather, of the M1907 model and the bayonet and bayonet scabbard are of the M1917 model.

5. DATA.

Gage of bore	12
Boring of barrel—riot type	Cylinder
Boring of barrel—skeet type	Improved cylinder
Boring of barrel—sporting type	Full choke
Type of action	Slide
Type of firing mechanism	Hammer
Type of magazine	Tubular
Capacity of magazine	5 rounds
Length of barrel—riot type	20 in.
Length of barrel—skeet type	26 in.
Length of barrel—sporting type	30 in.
Length of stock and receiver (approx.)	19½ in.
Length of assembled gun—riot type (approx.)	39 in.
Length of assembled gun—skeet type (approx.)	45 in.
Length of assembled gun—sporting type (approx.)	49 in.
Weight of assembled gun—riot type (approx.)	8 lb
Weight of assembled gun—skeet type (approx.)	7⅜ lb
Weight of assembled gun—sporting type (approx.)	7⅝ lb

ORDNANCE MAINTENANCE, SHOTGUNS, ALL TYPES

6. OPERATION.

a. The gun is operated by moving the action slide handle smartly and fully, backward and forward. This action unlocks the breech bolt, extracts and ejects the fired shell, cocks the hammer, transfers a live shell from the magazine to the chamber of the barrel and relocks the breech bolt behind the shell.

CAUTION: During operation, the muzzle of the gun should always be pointing at a safe spot.

b. Before the action slide can be retracted, the action slide lock must be disengaged from the action slide bar. If the gun has been fired, and the hammer consequently forward (down), the only movement necessary is to move the action slide handle forward slightly to allow the lock to disengage and then reciprocate it as above, as the descending hammer has already partly disengaged the lock. If the hammer is at half cock it must be pulled back to full cock, and the action slide lock release plunger pin then pressed and the handle pushed forward and reciprocated, as explained. If the gun is at full cock, proceed as just stated.

CAUTION: During these operations the finger should remain outside the trigger guard. Reciprocation of the slide handle should be full and smart to insure extraction of the shell, cocking of the hammer and complete locking of the breech bolt, and blocking of the action slide. Slamming of the mechanism should be avoided. When the gun is being fired as a repeater, all pressure should be removed from trigger while operating.

c. When the gun is being fired as a repeater, the recoil of the gun performs the preliminary forward movement of the action slide handle, as the gun recoils away from the handle, which is held by the operator.

d. With the gun loaded and locked and the hammer at full cock, the only operation necessary to fire the gun is to pull the trigger.

e. **To Load and Unload the Magazine.**

(1) To load the magazine press a shell, nose first, into the rear of the magazine against the magazine follower until the shell-stops, at the mouth of the magazine, snap out behind and retain the shell. Load another in the same way until five in all are loaded. Loading should be done with breech bolt locked and hammer at half cock.

(2) To unload the magazine, press in the two shell-stop plungers projecting through the walls of the receiver, and allow the shells to run out of the magazine. Inspect magazine to see that it is empty. Then operate the gun, if fully loaded, to extract and eject the shell in the chamber. Inspect chamber and receiver to be sure gun is empty.

CAUTION: Never let hammer fully down when there is a live shell in the chamber. To release action slide lock, retract hammer to full cock and, with fingers outside trigger guard, press lock release plunger pin, and retract slide as directed in b above.

WINCHESTER SHOTGUN, 12-GAGE, M97

f. To Load and Unload the Gun.

(1) To load a shell from the magazine into the chamber, pull back hammer to full cock, press action slide lock release plunger pin, and reciprocate action slide, as explained. Then let hammer down to half cock (safe) position. To load the chamber only with magazine empty, retract action slide, place shell directly in chamber of barrel through ejection opening in receiver, lock breech bolt, and place hammer at half cock. Check locking of breech bolt by attempting to retract the action slide. The action slide should not retract.

(2) To unload the gun, place hammer at half cock, unload magazine, and then place hammer at full cock, press action slide lock release plunger pin, and retract action slide to extract and eject shell in chamber. Then inspect magazine and chamber to be sure gun is completely unloaded.

CAUTION: To let hammer down from full to half cock, hold hammer firmly with thumb, press trigger, and ease hammer down slightly beyond half cock position; then pull it back until it definitely clicks into position, before releasing. Release trigger as soon as hammer is released from full cock.

7. FUNCTIONING.

a. As already briefly explained, the functioning of the operating mechanism is accomplished by the reciprocation of the action slide handle. A cam lug on the rear end of the action slide bar (fig. 3) engages in an irregular camming aperture in the left side of the carrier, and as the slide is moved backward, the carrier is cammed down; as the slide is moved forward, the carrier is cammed up.

b. The action slide hook, pivoted on the left side of the breech bolt (fig. 3), engages with the rear end of the action slide bar; and as the bar is reciprocated, the bolt is likewise moved back and forth. The timing of the movements of the carrier and bolt is such that the carrier is cammed completely up as the bolt reaches the extreme forward position. The locking shoulder on the forward end of the carrier is positioned behind the locking shoulder on the forward end of the bolt, thus locking the bolt in the closed position. As the bolt is locked in position, the action slide lock pivoted in the left side of the carrier springs out to block the rear end of the action slide bar. The action slide is thus prevented from moving to the rear and unlocking the bolt until the lock is disengaged either by the descending hammer, when the gun is fired, or by manual depression of the action slide lock release plunger pin extending through the right side of the receiver.

c. The breech bolt cams back and cocks the hammer as it moves to the rear. The hammer and sear are positioned in the rear end of the

ORDNANCE MAINTENANCE, SHOTGUNS, ALL TYPES

carrier. The hammer is released by retraction of the trigger mounted below it, which disengages the sear from the sear notch in the hammer. The firing pin is cammed back into the breech bolt by the firing pin lock as the carrier unlocks the bolt. The pin is held thus until the bolt is again locked, when it is released by a projection on the carrier pressing on and disengaging the lock to free the firing pin.

d. The carrier depresses the shell-stops positioned in the receiver directly behind the magazine on its downward movement, thus releasing a shell from the magazine, and at the same time takes over the function of the stops by blocking the next shell in the magazine. As the carrier rises to lock the bolt, it again releases the stops and they spring out to block the shell the carrier has been blocking. The released shell is pushed into the receiver by the force of the magazine spring and lifted to chamber level by the carrier in its upward movement. The breech bolt pushes the shell into the chamber on its forward movement and is locked behind it, as already explained. The shell guide, pivoted on the carrier, is cam-operated by the head of the action slide hook screw to clear the ejection opening in the receiver when the bolt is retracted.

e. The shell is extracted from the chamber by the extractors positioned in the forward end of the breech bolt, as the bolt moves to the rear, and is knocked out through the ejection opening in the right side of the receiver by the ejector positioned in the left inner wall of the receiver.

8. DISASSEMBLY AND ASSEMBLY (fig. 6).

a. Clean all parts thoroughly, oil lightly, and lubricate gun where necessary before assembling.

b. Bayonet Attachment and Hand Guard (fig. 4).

(1) DISASSEMBLY. Remove the three transverse clamp screws from the bayonet attachment and drive bayonet attachment and hand guard forward off muzzle end of barrel.

(2) ASSEMBLY. Assemble in reverse order.

c. Barrel, Magazine and Action Slide Group (Solid Frame Type) (fig. 4).

(1) DISASSEMBLY.

(a) Remove magazine stop screw from forward right side of receiver and unscrew magazine from receiver, using special spanner.

(b) The barrel should not be removed except for replacement. To remove, clamp receiver in vise with protected jaws and unscrew barrel, using a strap wrench.

(2) ASSEMBLY. Assemble in reverse order. Be sure to drop hammer and push carrier fully upward before pushing action slide bar back into receiver.

TM 9-1285
8

WINCHESTER SHOTGUN, 12-GAGE, M97

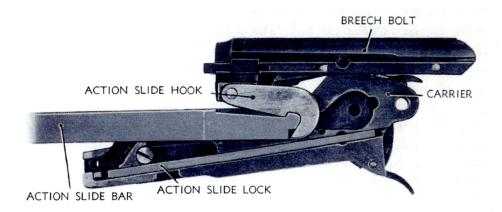

Breech Bolt Unlocked from Carrier — Action Slide Lock Disengaged

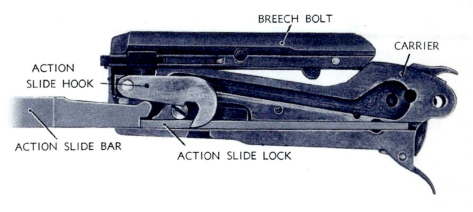

Breech Bolt Locked by Carrier — Action Slide Lock Engaged

Figure 3 — Breech Bolt, Carrier and Action Slide Bar Groups — Winchester Shotgun M97

d. Barrel, Magazine and Action Slide Group (Take-Down Type) (fig. 5).

(1) REMOVAL.

(a) Push downward on the magazine locking pin in the front end of the magazine and turn the magazine ¼ turn to the right.

(b) Force the action slide handle fully forward to disengage slide and magazine from receiver and turn barrel ¼ turn to the right.

(c) Pull barrel and magazine forward out of receiver.

TM 9-1285
8

ORDNANCE MAINTENANCE, SHOTGUNS, ALL TYPES

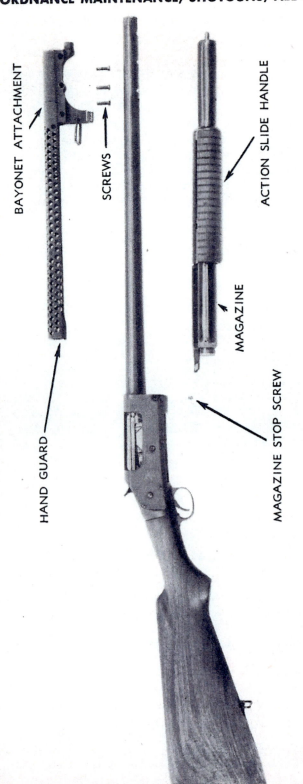

Figure 4—Bayonet Attachment, Magazine and Action Slide Groups Disassembled from Gun—Winchester Shotgun M97—Riot Type (Solid Frame)

WINCHESTER SHOTGUN, 12-GAGE, M97

(2) REPLACEMENT. Assemble in reverse order. Be sure to drop hammer and push carrier fully upward before pushing action slide bar back into receiver. Inspect bore for foreign matter before replacing barrel.

e. Carrier.

(1) REMOVAL.

(a) With barrel, magazine and action slide group removed, remove carrier pin stop screw from left rear top of carrier.

(b) Drop hammer and pry carrier fully downward to disengage it from breech bolt, using screwdriver inserted between carrier and breech bolt from right side.

(c) Cock the hammer and push out carrier pin laterally from rear end of receiver.

(d) Remove shell guide, stop screw from rear right side of receiver, and pull carrier downward out of receiver.

NOTE: Action slide group must be removed from magazine tube of solid frame gun before carrier can be removed.

(2) REPLACEMENT. Replace by assembling in reverse order.

f. Breech Bolt.

(1) REMOVAL. With carrier removed, remove action slide hook screw from forward right side of breech bolt, and draw breech bolt to the rear, out of receiver. Then remove slide hook from receiver.

(2) REPLACEMENT. Replace by assembling in reverse order. Allow head of slide hook screw to project not less than $\frac{1}{32}$ inch to act as cam for shell guide positioned on right side of carrier.

(3) DISASSEMBLY OF BREECH BOLT.

(a) Remove firing pin lock screw from left side of breech bolt and lift out firing pin lock and firing pin lock spring.

(b) Drive out firing pin stop pin from left to right and withdraw firing pin.

(c) To remove left-hand extractor, drive pin downward out of breech bolt and remove extractor.

(d) To remove right-hand extractor, insert a flat thin blade, such as a penknife or small screwdriver, between rear of extractor and extractor plunger and pry out extractor from breech bolt. Then lift out plunger and spring.

(4) ASSEMBLY OF BREECH BOLT. Assemble in reverse order.

g. Butt Stock.

(1) REMOVAL. The butt stock may be removed by first removing butt plate on rear end of butt stock and then, with long handle screw-

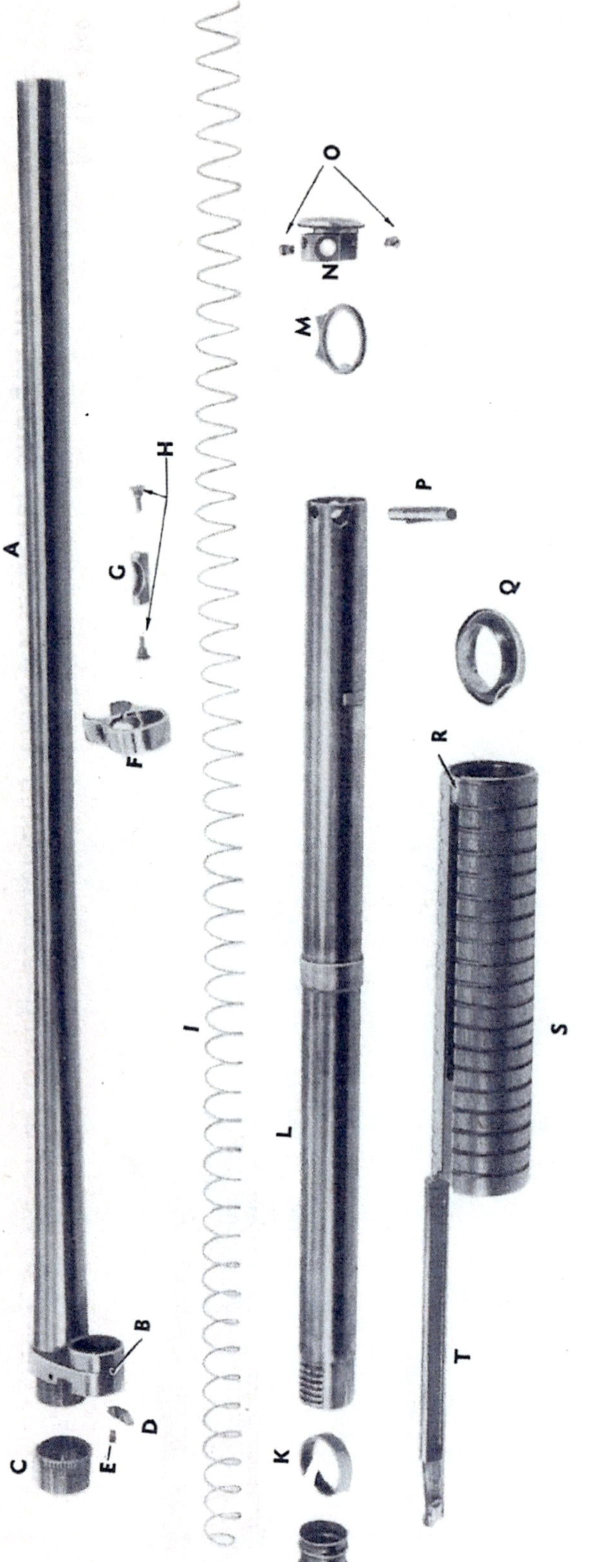

TM 9-1285
8

ORDNANCE MAINTENANCE, SHOTGUNS, ALL TYPES

A — BARREL
B — RECEIVER EXTENSION
C — BARREL ADJUSTING SLEEVE
D — BARREL ADJUSTING SLEEVE LOCK
E — BARREL ADJUSTING SLEEVE LOCK SCREW
F — MAGAZINE BAND
G — MAGAZINE BAND BUSHING
H — MAGAZINE BAND BUSHING SCREW
I — MAGAZINE SPRING
J — MAGAZINE FOLLOWER
K — ACTION SLIDE SPRING
L — MAGAZINE TUBE
M — MAGAZINE PLUG STOP
N — MAGAZINE PLUG
O — MAGAZINE PLUG SCREW
P — MAGAZINE LOCKING PIN AND SPRING
Q — ACTION SLIDE SLEEVE SCREW CAP
R — ACTION SLIDE SLEEVE
S — ACTION SLIDE HANDLE
T — ACTION SLIDE BAR

RA PD 40541

Figure 5 — Barrel, Magazine and Action Slide Group — Disassembled View — Winchester Shotgun M97 — (Take-Down)

TM 9-1285

WINCHESTER SHOTGUN, 12-GAGE, M97

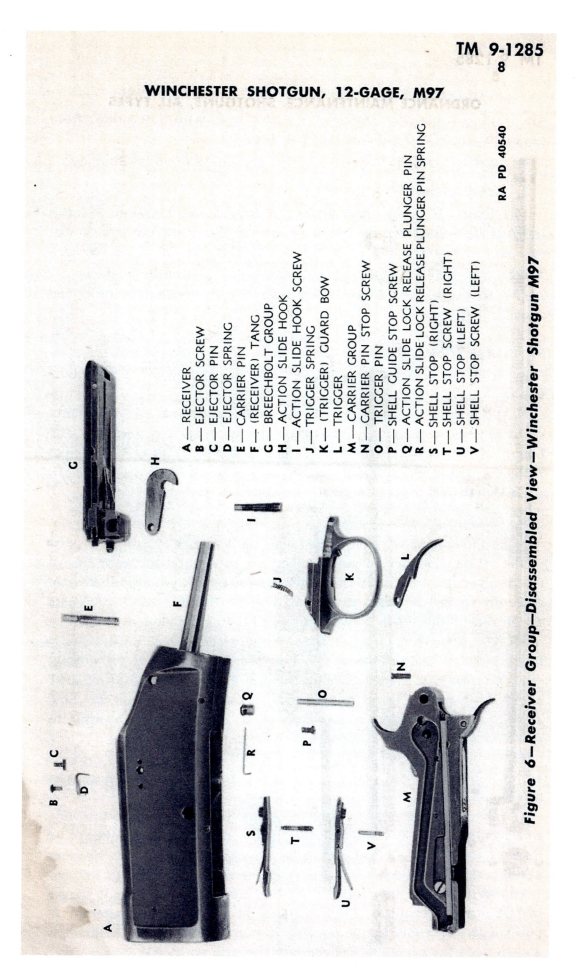

A — RECEIVER
B — EJECTOR SCREW
C — EJECTOR PIN
D — EJECTOR SPRING
E — CARRIER PIN
F — (RECEIVER) TANG
G — BREECHBOLT GROUP
H — ACTION SLIDE HOOK
I — ACTION SLIDE HOOK SCREW
J — TRIGGER SPRING
K — (TRIGGER) GUARD BOW
L — TRIGGER
M — CARRIER GROUP
N — CARRIER PIN STOP SCREW
O — TRIGGER PIN
P — SHELL GUIDE STOP SCREW
Q — ACTION SLIDE LOCK RELEASE PLUNGER PIN
R — ACTION SLIDE LOCK RELEASE PLUNGER PIN SPRING
S — SHELL STOP (RIGHT)
T — SHELL STOP SCREW (RIGHT)
U — SHELL STOP (LEFT)
V — SHELL STOP SCREW (LEFT)

RA PD 40540

Figure 6 — Receiver Group — Disassembled View — Winchester Shotgun M97

driver, unscrewing butt stock bolt (visible in hole in butt stock) from tang of receiver, and withdrawing butt stock to rear.

(2) REPLACEMENT. Replace by reversing procedure described above.

h. Trigger Guard.

(1) REMOVAL. The trigger guard and trigger may be removed, after the butt stock has been removed, by driving out guard pin from lower rear end of receiver and pulling guard to the rear from the receiver. Trigger and trigger spring and stop screw may then be removed.

(2) REPLACEMENT. Replace by reversing the procedure described above.

9. FIELD INSPECTION.

a. With gun completely assembled, test mechanism for proper functioning.

NOTE: Fired shells may often be used for testing, where dummy shells are not available, by turning in the uncrimped end so that the length of the shell approximates that of a live cartridge. Use of live shells for testing is prohibited.

CAUTION: Be sure gun is fully unloaded before inspection.

b. Operate the gun as follows:

(1) With the breech bolt locked, and the hammer at full cock, press in the action slide lock release plunger pin, located on the right side of the receiver. Push action slide handle forward slightly and pull smartly and fully to the rear; then push smartly and fully forward. Reciprocate action slide in this manner several times to test smoothness of action.

NOTE: Movement of action slide should be smart and full both ways to insure full cocking of hammer, locking of breech bolt, and engagement of action slide lock. Slamming of mechanism, however, should be avoided.

(2) Let hammer down to half cock, press release plunger pin, and attempt to retract action slide as above. It should not be possible to retract action slide.

(3) Retract hammer slightly to clear sear, retract trigger, and ease hammer down to fired position and repeat test as in (1) above. The action slide should retract.

(4) Retract slide as in (1) above, release plunger pin and push slide smartly and fully forward to lock the breech bolt. Then attempt to retract action slide. It should not be possible to do so with hammer at full cock until action slide lock is disengaged as in (1) and (2) above.

(5) With breech bolt locked and hammer at full cock, pull trigger to test firing mechanism. Place hammer at half cock and attempt to pull trigger. It should not be possible to pull trigger. (When hammer is at half cock the firing mechanism is in the safe position).

WINCHESTER SHOTGUN, 12-GAGE, M97

(6) With hammer at full cock, close but do not lock the breech bolt. Then attempt to fire the gun. The gun should not fire until the breech bolt is locked.

(7) Place two or more dummy or fired shells in the magazine and work through the action to test gun for feeding, loading, extraction and ejection of shells. The second shell should not leave the magazine until after the carrier has dropped as the first shell is being ejected.

NOTE: Fired shells will not work through the action as easily as live or dummy shells as they are somewhat deformed through being fired. Therefore, allowance should be made for friction and smoothness of action in positioning the shell.

c. If gun does not operate and function smoothly and properly when tested as above, damaged or improperly assembled parts are indicated as follows:

(1) ACTION SLIDE STICKS. May be due to bent slide bar, burs on bar cam lug, foreign matter in carrier camming aperture, or burs on breech bolt guideways or guides.

(2) BREECH BOLT DOES NOT LOCK. May be due to foreign matter on face of bolt or in extractor cuts in barrel, behind locking shoulder of bolt or on carrier, or worn or burred action slide bar cam lug.

(3) HAMMER DOES NOT COCK PROPERLY, OR SLIPS. May be due to burs or foreign matter in sear notches, burred sear nose, weak or broken sear spring, or foreign matter between trigger and sear.

(4) FIRING PIN DOES NOT RETRACT IN BREECH BOLT. May be due to broken or missing lock spring, foreign matter in breech bolt or broken parts.

(5) ACTION SLIDE LOCK DOES NOT FUNCTION. May be due to foreign matter under lock, broken lock or lock spring, burs on lock or action slide bar. Refer to the caution, paragraph 3 **j.**

(6) SHELL IS NOT EXTRACTED OR EJECTED. May be due to broken or worn extractors, ejector, or broken spring.

(7) TWO SHELLS FED INTO RECEIVER AT ONCE. May be due to broken shell-stop or springs, or foreign matter under stops.

(8) SHELLS STICK IN MAGAZINE. May be due to corroded or bent follower, dented tube, broken or kinked spring, or foreign matter in tube.

d. Inspect barrel and test trigger pull as prescribed in paragraph 3 **h** and **i**.

10. MAINTENANCE AND REPAIR.

a. **Burs on Camming Surfaces.** Burs on camming surfaces should be removed with a fine-grained sharpening stone. Care should be observed

ORDNANCE MAINTENANCE, SHOTGUNS, ALL TYPES

to stone evenly and lightly, remove as little metal as possible, and to maintain the angle of the face stoned. This is very important in the case of the action slide bar and slide lock; also the nose of the sear, and sear notches in the hammer. Such stoning should be done only by experienced ordnance personnel. Where parts are badly worn, they should be replaced.

b. Rust and Corrosion.

(1) Gun should be kept free of rust and corrosion at all times. Light rust may usually be removed with an oily rag or one moistened with **CLEANER**, rifle bore. If this method does not suffice, **CLOTH**, crocus, or **WOOL**, steel, fine, may be used. Care should be exercised to prevent undue scratching of surfaces.

(2) Rusting or leading of the bore of the barrel may occur. Rust usually appears in dark irregular patches; while leading shows in dull gray streaks. Leading is due to small quantity of lead from the shot pellets adhering to rough spots on the inner surface of the barrel. Leading seldom occurs when chilled shot is used. Rust or leading may be removed with a wad of **WOOL**, steel, fine, on the end of a cleaning rod. The wool should be pushed the full length of the bore each time and on a bore line, and not turned, or the bore scrubbed. This method prevents scratching the barrel which hastens fouling.

c. Stripped Threads in Wood of Stock. When wood screws strip out, they may be reset by boring out, plugging, reboring the stripped hole, and reseating the screw.

d. Cracks in Stock or Action Slide Handle. Small wood cracks may often be checked by boring a small hole just ahead of the crack and plugging with shellac or plastic wood. Do not use wooden plug. If crack is extensive, part should be replaced.

e. Loose Barrel (Take-Down Type Gun) (fig. 7). In the take-down type gun, if the barrel and magazine group become loose at the point where they mate with the receiver, they may be tightened as follows:

(1) Remove adjusting sleeve lock screw from right rear face of receiver extension and slide back and disengage adjusting sleeve lock from adjusting sleeve.

(2) Turn back the adjusting sleeve one notch, engage lock with sleeve, and replace lock screw.

(3) If barrel is still loose when assembled, repeat the operation until tight.

f. Worn or broken parts should be replaced by new parts and the gun tested for operation and functioning upon assembly.

WINCHESTER SHOTGUN, 12-GAGE, M97

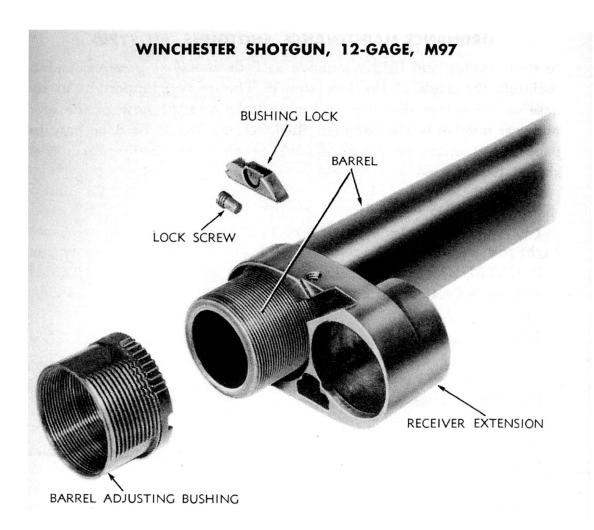

Figure 7 — Barrel Adjusting Sleeve Disassembled — Winchester Shotgun M97 — (Take-Down)

11. CLEANING AND LUBRICATION.

a. Cleaning the Bore.

(1) Barrels of take-down type guns should be removed from the receiver when cleaning the bore. Barrels of solid frame guns may be cleaned from the breech end of the receiver when the breech bolt and carrier have been removed, or from the muzzle end. If bores of solid frame guns are badly rusted or corroded, the gun should be completely disassembled and the barrel thoroughly cleaned.

(2) The bore should be thoroughly cleaned with CLEANER, rifle bore, or soap and water solution (issue soap) applied to a cloth patch assembled to the cleaning rod, then thoroughly dried and lightly oiled with OIL, lubricating, preservative, light.

CAUTION: All oil should be removed from bore and chamber before firing the gun.

b. Cleaning Parts Other Than the Bore.

(1) When overhauling gun, before assembling parts or groups, the

ORDNANCE MAINTENANCE, SHOTGUNS, ALL TYPES

parts should be thoroughly cleaned and lightly oiled with OIL, lubricating, preservative, light. If necessary, groups and assemblies should be disassembled to accomplish thorough cleaning and oiling.

(2) Cleaning is best accomplished by wiping parts with a rag slightly moistened with CLEANER, rifle bore, or light oil, to loosen burnt powder and like foreign matter. Then wipe clean with clean dry rag and oil lightly, using rag lightly moistened with OIL, lubricating, preservative, light.

(3) Special attention should be paid to cam and guide grooves, spring seats, firing pin aperture, and like apertures where foreign matter may become lodged and caked and prevent proper functioning of the mechanism.

(4) Wood parts of stock and action slide handle may be cleaned by wiping with slightly oily rag and then polishing with clean dry rag. Light application of OIL, linseed, applied with a rag and well rubbed into the wood with the heel of the hand, will help to preserve the wood. This treatment is only effective on wood parts with an oil finish. Varnished wood should be cleaned with a lightly oiled rag, using light lubricating oil, and then polished with a clean dry cloth. Care should be observed to prevent OIL, linseed, from getting into mechanism of gun, as it will become gummy when dry.

(5) The magazine tube, spring, and follower should be cleaned and lightly oiled to prevent rusting. Excess oil should be avoided as it is apt to soak into shells, affecting the charge, or be carried into the chamber of the barrel, thus increasing breech pressure at this point.

c. Lubrication.

(1) Lubrication should be kept to a minimum, as too much oil attracts foreign matter and burnt powder which will become caked and cause stoppage or undue wear in the mechanism. Lubricating is best accomplished by using an oiler with a small nose, or a dropper, by which the direction and amount of oil used can be controlled.

(2) Points to lubricate are:

(a) Action slide bar opening in forward end of receiver.

(b) Action slide bar cam lug.

(c) Action slide lock.

(d) Carrier pin.

(e) Breech bolt guides.

(f) Outer surface of magazine tube where action slide handle (tube) bears.

(g) Action slide hook screw.

(h) Hammer pin.

(i) Action slide lock release, in carrier.

WINCHESTER SHOTGUN, 12-GAGE, M97

(3) In very cold climates, oiling and lubrication should be reduced to a minimum. Only surfaces showing signs of wear should be lightly oiled.

d. Preparation of Shotguns for Storage.

(1) OIL, lubricating, preservative, light, is the most suitable oil for preserving the mechanism of shotguns. This oil is efficient for preserving the polished surfaces, the bore, and the chamber for a period of from 2 to 6 weeks, dependent on the climatic and storage conditions. Shotguns in short term storage should be inspected every 5 days and the preservative film renewed, if necessary.

(2) COMPOUND, rust-preventive, light, is a semisolid material. This compound is efficient for preserving the polished metal surfaces, the bore, and the chamber for a period of one year or less, dependent on the climatic and storage conditions.

(3) The shotguns should be cleaned and prepared with particular care. The bore, all parts of the mechanism, and the exterior of the shotguns should be thoroughly cleaned and then dried completely with rags. In damp climates, particular care must be taken to see that the rags are dry. After drying a metal part, the bare hands should not touch that part. All metal parts should then be coated either with OIL, lubricating, preservative, light, or COMPOUND, rust-preventive, light, depending on the length of storage ((1) and (2) above). Application of the COMPOUND, rust-preventive, to the bore of the shotgun is best done by dipping the cleaning brush in COMPOUND, rust-preventive, light, and running it through the bore two or three times. (Cleaning brush must be clean.) Before placing the shotgun in the packing chest, see that the bolt is in its forward position and that the hammer is released. Then, handling the shotgun by the wooden parts only, it should be placed in the packing chest, the wooden supports at the butt and muzzle having previously been painted with COMPOUND, rust-preventive, light. Under no circumstances should a shotgun be placed in storage contained in a cloth or other cover, or with a plug in the bore. Such articles collect moisture which causes the weapon to rust.

NOTE: If shotguns are packed in cardboard containers or original manufacturer's cartons, each gun (or section of gun, if taken down) should be wrapped in greaseproof paper after preparing for storage.

e. Cleaning of Shotguns as Received from Storage.

(1) Shotguns which have been stored in accordance with subparagraph d above, will be coated with either OIL, lubricating, preservative, light, or COMPOUND, rust-preventive, light. Shotguns received from ordnance storage will, in general, be coated with COMPOUND, rust-preventive, heavy. Use SOLVENT, dry-cleaning, to remove all traces of the compound or oil, particular care being taken that all recesses in

which springs or plungers operate, trigger mechanisms and slide lock groups or similar parts, are cleaned thoroughly. After using the SOLVENT, dry-cleaning, make sure it is completely removed from all parts. Then oil, as described in paragraph 11. If guns are to be used immediately, bore and chamber should be wiped dry of oil or grease, and excess oil removed from exterior surfaces with a dry rag.

NOTE: Failure to clean the firing pin and the recess in the bolt in which it operates, the slide lock and trigger mechanism or similar groups, may result in gun failure at normal temperatures, and will most certainly result in serious malfunctions if the shotguns are operated in low temperature areas, as COMPOUND, rust-preventive, and other foreign matter will cause the lubricating oil to congeal or frost on the mechanism.

(2) SOLVENT, dry-cleaning, is an inflammable and noncorrosive petroleum distillate used for removing oil and COMPOUND, rust-preventive. Its use is prohibited near open flame and where smoking is permitted. It is generally applied with rag swabs to large parts and as a bath for small parts. The surfaces must be thoroughly dried immediately after removal of the solvent. To avoid leaving finger marks, which are ordinarily acid and induce corrosion, gloves should be worn by persons handling parts after such cleaning. SOLVENT, dry-cleaning, will attack and discolor rubber.

f. Care and Cleaning in Cold Climates.

(1) In temperatures below freezing, it is necessary that the moving parts of the shotgun be kept absolutely free from moisture. It has also been found that excess oil on the working parts will solidify to such an extent as to cause sluggish operation or complete failure.

(2) The metal parts of the shotgun should be taken apart and completely cleaned with SOLVENT, dry-cleaning, before use in temperatures below 0 F. The working surfaces of parts which show signs of wear may be lubricated by rubbing with a cloth which has been wet with oil and wrung out. At temperatures above 0 F, the shotgun may be oiled lightly after cleaning by wiping with a slightly oiled cloth, using OIL, lubricating, preservative, light.

(3) Immediately upon bringing indoors, the shotgun should be allowed to come to room temperature. It should be disassembled, wiped completely dry of condensed moisture, and oiled with OIL, lubricating, preservative, light.

(a) If shotgun has been fired, it should be thoroughly cleaned and oiled. The bore may be swabbed out with an oily patch and when the weapon reaches room temperature, thoroughly cleaned and oiled as prescribed in paragraph 11.

(b) Before firing, the shotgun should be cleaned and oil removed as

WINCHESTER SHOTGUN, 12-GAGE, M97

prescribed in **f** (2) above. The bore and chamber should be entirely free of oil before firing.

g. Care and Cleaning in Hot Climates.

(1) TROPICAL CLIMATES.

(a) In tropical climates where temperatures and humidity are high, or where salt air is present, and during rainy seasons, the shotgun should be thoroughly inspected at frequent intervals and kept lightly oiled when not in use. The groups should be dismounted at regular intervals and, if necessary, disassembled to enable the drying and oiling of parts.

(b) Care should be exercised to see that unexposed parts and surfaces are kept clean and oiled, such as the underside of the barrel, magazine tube, interior of receiver and operating parts, spring wells and like parts and surfaces. The inside of magazine tube, spring, and follower should be inspected occasionally and kept lightly oiled.

(c) In hot climates, OIL, lubricating, preservative, light, should be used for lubrication.

(d) Wood parts should also be inspected to see that swelling due to moisture does not bind working parts. In such cases, shave off wood only enough to relieve binding. A light coat of OIL, linseed, raw, applied at intervals and well rubbed in, with the heel of the hand, will help to keep out moisture. Allow oil to soak in for a few hours and then wipe and polish wood with dry clean rag. OIL, linseed, raw, should only be used on wooden parts having an oil finish (not varnished).

NOTE: Care should be taken that OIL, linseed, raw, does not get into mechanism or on metal parts as it will become gummy when dry.

(2) HOT, DRY CLIMATES.

(a) In hot dry climates where sand and dust are apt to get into the mechanism and bore, the shotgun should be wiped clean daily, or oftener, if necessary. Groups should be dismounted and disassembled as far as necessary to facilitate thorough cleaning.

(b) Oiling and lubrication should be kept to a minimum, as oil will collect dust which will act as an abrasive on the working parts and foul the bore and chamber. OIL, lubricating, preservative, light, is best for lubrication where temperatures are high, and should be lightly applied only to the surfaces of working parts showing signs of wear.

(c) In such climates, wood parts are apt to dry out and shrink, and a light application of OIL, linseed, raw, applied as in paragraph g (1) *(d)* above, will help to keep wood in condition.

(d) Perspiration from the hands is a contributing factor to rust on account of acid present in perspiration, and metal parts should be wiped dry frequently.

(e) During sand or dust storms, the gun should be kept covered, if possible, especially the receiver openings.

Made in the USA
Monee, IL
10 November 2020